I0762654

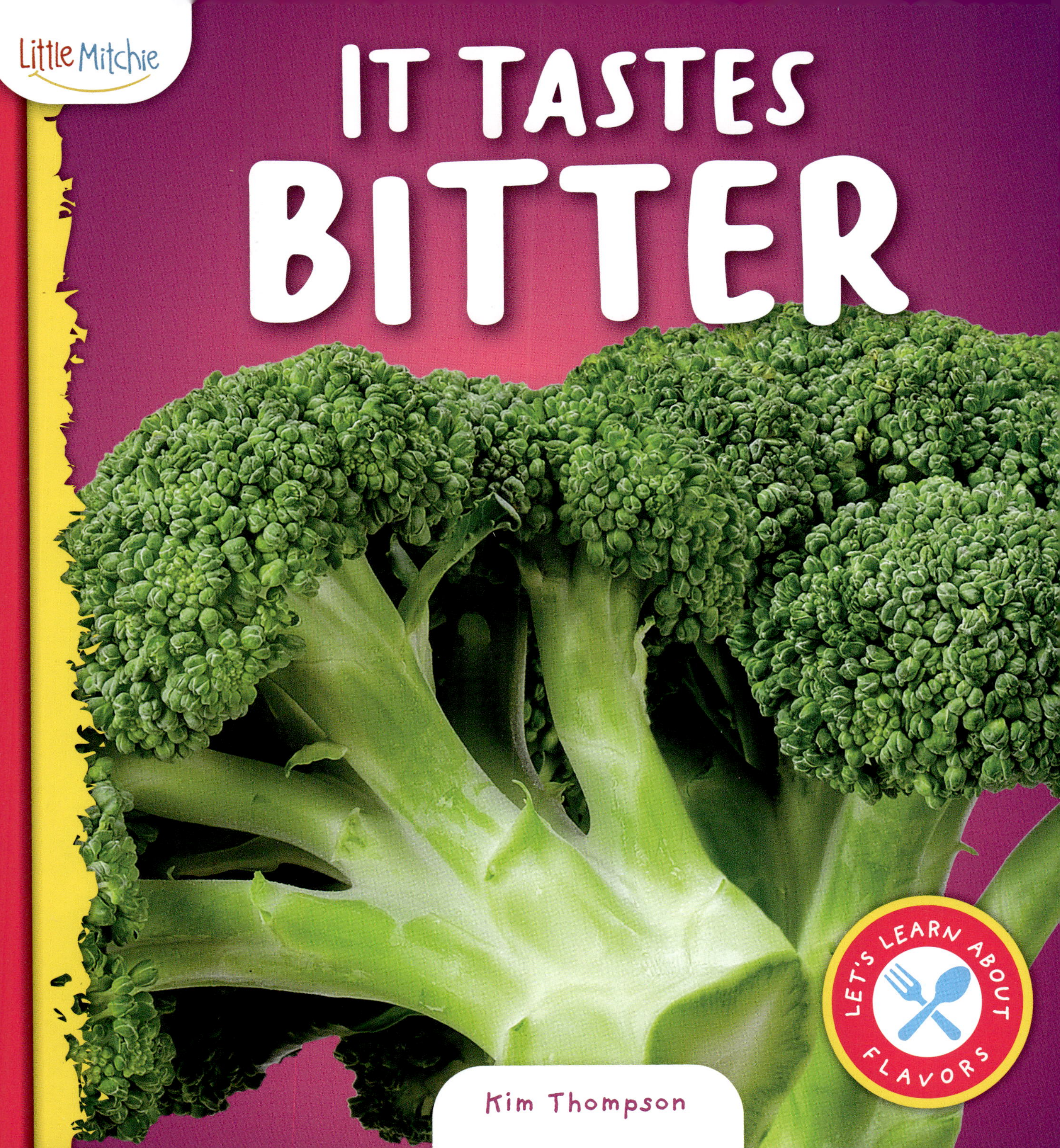
Little Mitchie
IT TASTES
BITTER
LET'S LEARN ABOUT FLAVORS
Kim Thompson

CREATING YOUNG NONFICTION READERS

Little Mitchie books spark curiosity and support early nonfiction reading for students in Grades 2-3. Designed to build vocabulary, support second language learners, and prepare readers for middle-grade content, each book includes helpful tips for parents and educators to build confidence and deepen understanding of the world.

TIPS FOR READING NONFICTION WITH BEGINNING READERS

Talk about Nonfiction

Begin by explaining that nonfiction books give us information that is true. The book will be organized around a specific topic or idea, and we may learn new facts through reading.

Look at the Parts

Most nonfiction books have helpful features. Our *Little Mitchie* titles include color photographs and graphic aids, a table of contents, a glossary, and an index. Share the purpose of these features with your reader.

Color Photos and Graphic Aids

A lot of information can be found by "reading" photos, charts, maps, and other graphic aids found within nonfiction texts. Help your reader learn more about the different ways information can be displayed.

Table of Contents

Located at the front of the book, this list shows the big ideas within the text and the page numbers where they can be found.

Glossary

Located at the back of the book, the glossary defines key words and phrases that are related to the topic. These words and phrases can be found in the text in colored type.

Index

Located at the back of the book, an index is an alphabetical list of topics and the page numbers where they can be found.

With a little help and guidance about reading nonfiction, you can feel good about introducing a young reader to the world of *Little Mitchie* nonfiction books.

Little Mitchie is an imprint of:

PUBLISHERS

2001 SW 31st Avenue
Hallandale, FL 33009
mitchelllanepub.com

First Edition, 2027.

Author: Kim Thompson
Designer: Bobbie Houser

Library of Congress Cataloging-in-Publication Data
Title: It Tastes Bitter / by Kim Thompson

Description: Hallandale, FL :
Mitchell Lane Publishers, [2027]

Identifiers:
ISBN 979-8-89260-854-1 (library bound)
ISBN 979-8-89260-951-7 (eBook)

Library of Congress Control Number: 2026935744

PHOTO CREDITS
Shutterstock: Khumthong, cover, 1, 3, 4, 10, 18; Tatjana Baibakova, 5; 12 Studio, 6; New Africa, 9, 19, 22; PeopleImages, 11; Vladimir Gjorgiev, 12; dr.Barmely, 14; Antonio Guillem, 15; Xavier Lorenzo, 17; Ground Picture, 20.

TABLE OF CONTENTS

Chapter One

A BITTER TASTE

Bite into a brussels sprout. Pop a tart cranberry in your mouth. Nibble on dark chocolate. Wash it all down with strong coffee. Each taste is sharp and **acrid**. It makes your eyes open wide!

These foods have different shapes, colors, and textures. They have one flavor in common, though. They are all bitter!

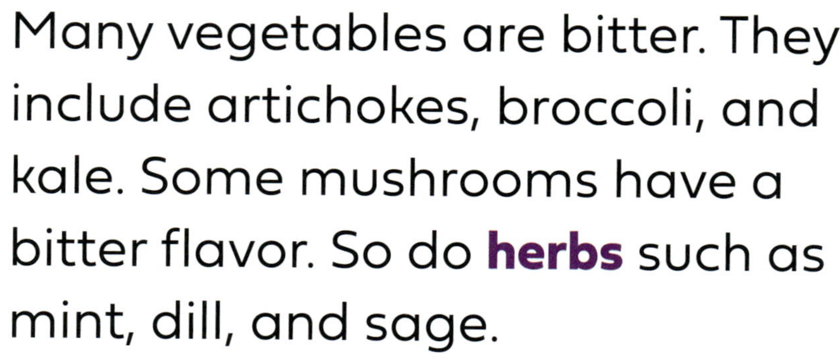

Many vegetables are bitter. They include artichokes, broccoli, and kale. Some mushrooms have a bitter flavor. So do **herbs** such as mint, dill, and sage.

TASTY TIDBIT

Bitter melon is green and bumpy. The cucumber-shaped melon has a very bitter taste.

Cacao beans and coffee beans are very bitter. People **ferment** them and roast them. They add other ingredients. They get the milder flavors of coffee, cocoa, and chocolate.

Chapter Two

THE SCIENCE OF BITTERNESS

Pungent, bitter tastes come from chemicals. Phenols, flavonoids, caffeine, and other chemicals are found in bitter foods.

These chemicals taste different to different people. **Genetics** plays a part. Some people are sensitive to bitter flavors. Some people can't taste them at all.

The surface of your tongue is covered with bumps called **papillae**. They are not taste buds. Your taste buds are tiny structures inside the papillae.

A taste bud is pocket-shaped. Tiny hairs called microvilli stick out. They sense chemicals found in bitter foods. **Signals** get sent to your brain. Then, you know you are tasting something bitter.

There are five flavors that can be detected by taste buds. They are bitter, sweet, salty, savory, and sour.

TASTY TIDBIT

It's not true that different areas of your tongue taste different flavors. All five flavors can be sensed all over your tongue.

Kids have more taste buds than adults. This may explain why many kids dislike bitter foods, and many adults like them. Most coffee drinkers are adults!

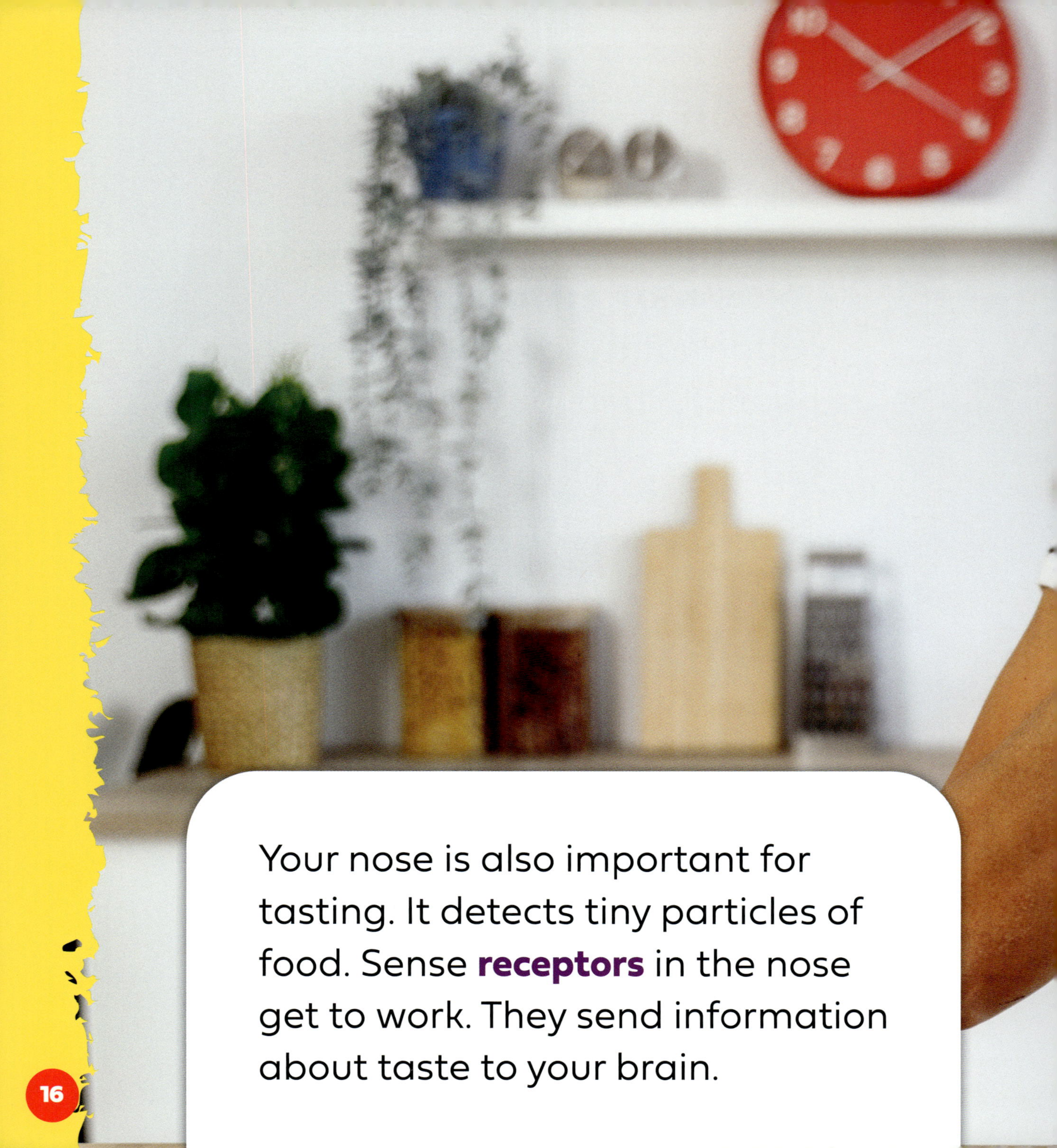

Your nose is also important for tasting. It detects tiny particles of food. Sense **receptors** in the nose get to work. They send information about taste to your brain.

Chapter Three

EATING BITTER FOODS

Tasting bitter flavors may help people avoid **toxins**. Many poisonous plants are bitter. If something tastes very bitter, your brain tells you to spit it out!

TASTY TIDBIT
Plants make toxins to keep animals (including humans!) from eating them. Then, animals develop the ability to eat the toxins. It's an endless cycle in nature.

But many bitter foods are healthy. They help prevent cancer. They are good for your heart, gut, and eyes.

Bitter foods are anything but boring. Try radishes with your ranch dip. Stir dark cocoa powder into your milk. Bitterness might make your food better!

BRILLIANTLY BITTER SMOOTHIE

Ingredients:

Fresh kale, small bundle

½ cup unsweetened apple juice

¼ cup plain yogurt

Ripe banana

½ cup frozen strawberries, blueberries, or raspberries

Directions:

1. Have an adult use a knife to remove the stems from the kale. You should have one cup of leafy greens.
2. With an adult, put the kale in a blender along with all other ingredients.
3. Blend until smooth.
4. Pour into a cup. Taste and enjoy! If the smoothie is too bitter, add a little honey or maple syrup.

GLOSSARY

acrid (A-kruhd) sharp, harsh, and often unpleasant

cacao beans (kuh-KOU beenz) the seeds of the cacao tree that are used to make cocoa and chocolate

ferment (fur-MENT) to use bacteria or yeast to break down the chemicals in a substance

genetics (juh-NET-iks) the way that characteristics and traits are passed from one generation to the next through genes

herbs (urbs) plants that are used to flavor foods and make medicines

papillae (puh-PILL-ee) small bumps on the tongue that contain taste buds

pungent (PUHN-juhnt) having a strong, sharp taste or smell

receptors (ri-SEP-turz) nerve endings that are sensitive to stimuli in the environment such as smells

signals (SIG-nuhlz) chemical and electrical messages that get sent to the brain through the body's nervous system

toxins (TAHK-sinz) poisons made by living things such as plants

FURTHER READING

Brown, Molly Meehan. *Herbal Activities for Kids: 50 Nature Crafts, Recipes, and Garden Projects.* Storey Publishing, 2024.

Highlights. *The Ultimate Science Cookbook for Kids: A Cookbook for Young Scientists That Transforms the Kitchen into a Food Lab for Learning.* Highlights Press, 2025.

ON THE INTERNET

Denver Museum of Nature and Science: The Five Tastes
youtube.com/watch?v=MZn2PMUWO-Y
Learn more about the five flavors your tongue can taste.

Healthline: Nine Bitter Foods That Are Good for You
healthline.com/nutrition/bitter-foods
Learn about healthy bitter foods you may want to try.

INDEX